The Great Canopy

by

Paula Goldman

Gival Press

Arlington, Virginia

Published by Gival Press, an imprint of Gival Press, LLC.

For information please write:
Gival Press, LLC, P. O. Box 3812, Arlington, VA 22203.

Website: www.givalpress.com

First edition ISBN 1-928589-31-6
Library of Congress Control Number: 2005931718

Cover art:
Georges Braque (French, 1882-1963), *House Behind Trees*, 1906-1907, Oil
on canvas. The Metropolitan Museum of Art, Robert Lehman Collection,
1975. (1975.1.159) Photograph © 1962 The Metropolitan Museum of Art.

Photo of Paula Goldman: Copyright © 2005 by Rick Thompson.
Format and design by Ken Schellenberg.

"The classics aren't dead: they're alive and well and living in Paula Goldman's poems. From Greek tragedy to Roman myth, from Madame Bovary to Renaissance painters, this poetic scavenger places us in the thoroughly modern context of family life with language as conversational and current as your last intimate phone call, yet in her poems flow the ageless currents of our joys and struggles and human triumphs. I'm sure you'll enjoy this delightful and moving collection."

—Roger Weingarten

"With chutzpah and often the blunt finality of a meat cleaver, this brilliant butcher's daughter skillfully transforms alternating personal and cultural pain into an ongoing opportunity for inner growth that, in turn, rises to the level of the great canopy of art. But, really, I treasure Paula Goldman's poems not just for the fact that they are 'art', but because they are fresh reminders of how complex, sensitively exquisite, and often heroically transcendent we everyday humans can be."

—Jack Myers, 2003 Texas Poet Laureate

Acknowledgments

The author wishes to express grateful acknowledgment to the following publications in which some of these poems first appeared:

"Atlantic City Snapshot, 1944" in *Boomer Girl, Poems by Women of the Baby Boom Generation,* edited by Pamela Gemin & Paula Sergi, University of Iowa Press, 1999.

"Downsizing" in *Harvard Review.*

"Adios, Caravaggio" in *Passages North*, Vol. 25, No. 1, Winter/Spring 2004.

"The Cunning of Edgar Degas," called "Edgar Degas," and "The Bather," in *Clockwatch Review, Vol. 8, Nos. 1 & 2, 1993.*

"The Fifth Wonder of the World" in *Poet Miscellany* 24, Summer 1995.

"Leda Redux" in *The G. W. Review,* Vol. 16, Nos. 1 & 2, Spring, 1996.

"O'Keeffe's Black Door" and "Michelangelo's Last Pietà" in *The Cream City Review*, Vol. 18, No. 1, Spring, 1994.

"In the Locker Room" and "True Stories" in *The Party Train, A Collection of North American Prose Poetry* edited by Robert Alexander, Mark Vinz, & C.W. Truesdale published by New Rivers Press, 1996.

"Burrowings from Bogan and Joyce: Unlikely Pairs" in *Clockwatch Review.* Vol. 7, Nos. 1 & 2, 1991, 1992.

"Waitressing" in *Midland Review,* No. 8, Spring 1992.

"The Other Side" in *Birmingham Poetry Review*, No. 12, Spring-Summer, 1994.

"Naked Companions," "Desire" and "The Long Married Life" in *Architrave: A Journal of the Arts,* Winter, 1996.

"Gaining" and "Pietà Rondanini" in *Kansas Quarterly,* Vol. 24 & 25, No. 1 4/92 & 1/93.

"The Weight of An Apple" in *Amelia*, No. 26, 1994.

"Wild Beasts" in *The Prose Poem, San Marcos, Prose Poetry by Women, 1994,* edited by Steve Wilson.

"Monet's Liquid Walls" in *Slant, VII, Summer, 1993.*

"Mammogram" appearing slightly differently in *Claiming the Spirit Within, A Sourcebook of Women's Poetry,* edited by Marilyn Sewell published by Beacon Press, 1996.

"Albert Giacometti's Wife" called "Giacometti's Large Seated Woman

1958" in *EKPHRASIS,* Vol. 1. No. 3, Spring /Summer, 1998.

"The Movie Version" in *River Oak Review,* No. 11, Fall, 1998.

"Almost a Love Poem" in *Poet Lore,* Vol. 89, No. 4, Winter 1994-95.

"In the Musée d'Orsay" INKWELL *Magazine's* 1997 first prize award.

"Dried Springs" 1998 *Louisiana Literature Prize for Poetry, Louisiana Literature, Vol. 15, No. 1 , Spring 1998.*

"Vivaldi and Oranges" semi-finalist award *Louisiana Literature Prize for Poetry, Louisiana Literature,* Vol. 15, No. 2, Fall, 1998.

"The Anointed," "Unloading the Carts, " and "Amazing Grace" (in slightly different form) in *Blue Mesa Review,* No. 5, Spring, 1993.

"The Change" and Man After His Bath" in *Bellevue Literary Review,* Volume 3 Number 2, Fall 2003.

"That Bitch Goddess" in *Poetic Voices Without Borders* edited by Robert L. Giron published by Gival Press, 2005.

"Earthly Paradise" in *Green Mountains Review,* Vol. 18, No. 1, Spring, 2005.

For Allan and in memory of my parents

I would like to give special thanks to Sara Talpos, whose probing questions aided many of these poems, and Richard Jackson, Jack Myers, Roger Weingarten, John Koethe, Laurie Winters, Kit Basquin, Renee Wolfson, for inspiration and careful readings along the way.

Contents

Part Three

Part One

Diana's Temple

Oh, please stay by me, Diana
— *Paul Anka*

I keep stumbling on stones,
        cold stumps of Europe,
                the base of this headless

column, an elephant's foot.
        I remember that trick,
                the trainer lies down

face up under the raised
        foot, the audience waiting,
                then disappointed. I

want to be anointed, arch
        against the Midi sky,
                let my arrows fly, lift

my callused heels, bleed a
        little. Two temple cats,
                marbleized, watch me.

I feel gypped, no altars
        are lit, it costs nothing
                to enter this temple. Listen.

Pigeons in the scaffolding,
        planks like the boardwalk in
                Atlantic City, where I chased

after Miss Massachusetts, who
        like a chaste Diana, waved
                from a yellow Buick

3

convertible, her gloved arms
    riding the night sky
        like a pair of mourning

doves heading for the Ferris
    wheel. Long nights of
        amusement piers, I

traipsed beside the FAT
    LADY— my lobotomized
        aunt, Chaplin look-alike

bookie, a gimp Russian
    butcher shouting after me.
        Those steel and iron

pilings reaching 1,780 feet,
    blasted from the water, hotels—
        dynamited. Pitted

and pocked, Diana's temple
    stock rises. Next door, condos
        go up, a crane towers

an umbrella pine. Everything
    has its price, just ask
        my old man, whose heavy

thumb pressed on the scale,
    selling kosher veal chops
        to Italians, asking

for pork. "What do they know?"
    he said. "Dumb *dagos*. And
        you're no Miss America."

The Family Romance

You cherished me, my mother,
But even you desert me.
I am sent to an empty place.
            —H.D.'s Iphigeneia in Aulis of Euripides

(1)

Iphigeneia's Neck

                    Still I was excited,
I'd never been away from home. A beach
holiday and a chance to see my father,
poor Agamemnon, always pushed around,
thinking he was in charge. Mother was
never satisfied, gladly sending him off
for gold. She had this thing for the hard
stuff, necklaces, combs, twisted ropes
for her dark hair. Helen wasn't the only
one who saw Paris streaking about. Mother
never liked her, pretty is skin-deep.
But I did, especially when she'd brush
my hair, promising *you'll grow up pretty,*
like me. Mother, when asked about such
things, patted my head, threw hers back
and laughed, *you'll pass*, all but nailing
my coffin, me, tender as a rabbit.

Klytemnestra Sees the Doctor

The sun looks away as I pass through
the Lioness Gate, a damp chill runs up
my sleeve. And when I pick up this conch
shell, a souvenir from the beach at Aulis,
I hear Iphigeneia's screams, see Agamemnon's
blood, the whore's, Cassandra's, ruining
the royal sheets, towels, tiles, a veritable
flood, who would have thought . . . all those
meat dishes, he couldn't get enough, killing
a daughter for a breeze. She's better off
marrying Death who betrays no one. I loved
a king before he was king, before his royal
neck was red and bullish. I used to watch him
shave, sit on the toilet seat, offer up
the squares of paper to stop up the blood
where he'd nicked himself. Often he'd give me
the razor, say *go ahead*. Here, doctor,
put your hand here, and feel the hatred
swelling, replacing the child I was.

Atlantic City Snapshot, 1944

Eight ladies walk arm in arm
uniformly jeweled and coiffured
under a billboard of a
Coppertone baby
above the boardwalk.
I am not born yet.

Mother wears a Persian lamb
coat, shoulder bag and black beaded
beret. Her dark gloved hand holds
the thin strap in place,
a hand that will not
soothe my tearful face.

Such a sad face Mother makes,
the gray photograph torn above
her head as if forked lightning
had struck her forlorn
on this bright day. She
never liked herself

in pictures. Shadows fall, point
to noon at Kentucky Ave.
and the boardwalk. I will buy
and sell properties
in Monopoly
over and over,

and lose to avaricious
brothers, but never will I part
with this dressup version of
Mother who wore blood-
stained aprons in a
kosher meat market.

Mother, who stunk of sweat, wears
black open toed shoes and (a dash
of Arpège) and her regrets
for the camera.
I smell the photo
for the ocean's salt

spray, but it's a different
ocean. I have not taken in
my first wave or plunged into
the hot sand, trembling
from the cold, my first
home, the Atlantic.

The boardwalk is the home of
the original salt water
taffy—Fralinger's. I try
to smell the candy
stores lining the boards
under the hotels

where Mother's walking. Hotels
built like sand castles span a time
before and after I am
born when Father goes
to jail for having
sold meat on the black

market, his name—*our name*—spread
on the front page of the A.C.
paper. No wonder Mother's
lips are pressed tightly
and her eyes look out
at the camera

hopelessly, but it took years
to find out—it wasn't my fault,
the sadness, I mean, and not
even my father's
business. It's before
I'm in the picture.

The Museum of Childhood

(Edinburgh, Scotland)

is shelf after shelf
of chalked faced dolls
in Havisham gowns
drawn by horseless
carriages past death
grinning marionettes
whose perfume fills
empty theater sets when
all the children are carried
to bed, dreaming of
parades, boxed Napoleon
armies marching out
at midnight over a necropolis
of nappies, plastic teats, tarnished
teething rings, Roy Rogers'
comics, cartoons of a mouse
from someone else's house
as my own dream winds
to a small pine wardrobe, its painted
rose on a door opening
to a pink organdy dress,
overalls, maybe a pair
of spotless Mary Jane's,
so small in that shoebox
of an apartment above
my father's store, the carnage
overheard between the overheated
customers and the hardened
butcher. As they haggled, I hugged
my Tiny Tears doll, her arms
snapped, the times my chest

heaved, wheezing, I called
and no one came, the mechanism
broke, I blinked and stared.

In the Name of the Wolf

after Vasko Popa

When I was born
They gave me to the arms
Of my grandmother Wolfson

As long as she lived she called
Me *shana maydela*
In her clotted Yiddish tongue

In the open she fed me
Raw hamburger so I would grow up
Not a weakling

I believed her
My eyes began to blossom
In the crib

My parents never heard me
Howl at the sky
Thinking it had fallen

Taffy

When he went to say something good— not
often— it was as if an angel, a bad one,
put a hand over his mouth or twisted
the words inside into a just
barely audible sound, "good for
nothing," "sonovabitch," "get lost," and you
skulked away, feeling as if you'd
done something, when all you wanted
was to show your drawing or a few words
scrawled on a pad, perhaps
spelling "Dad," you know that
yellow, blue lined paper, triple spaced,
handed out in first grade, leaving
the teacher plenty of room for corrections.
Let's start with the sneer, as if he'd
eaten a sour tomato at his mother's
table and couldn't get rid of it, or perhaps
manufactured too much bile, so that
later in life when he complained
of a bad taste, you weren't
surprised—bound to come out— he was
mean, and no amount of *taffying*, what
he called it, could change that.

In the Locker Room

Undressing I look down, see my belly and hate myself. Don't other women? I think of the *Venus of Willendorf,* her tiny arms over her breasts, her stomach a voluminous pouch. My book says, "she exudes pride and contentment." I see softness where I want to be as hard as Lady MacBeth's gallstones.

Rosa, the Argentine health director, passes and says, "Ah, Paula, suck it in." Here in the locker room, we're all bellyachers. In Ingres' *The Turkish Bath, 1862,* "a scene forbidden to the male gaze," the women are enjoying themselves, one clasping another's breast, one playing a lute, another dancing. They look a little dazed, like they've been smoking hashish.

And they all have soft bellies as round as their instruments. They seem at home in their bodies while I'm always out visiting. It's a circular composition. In the inner sanctum of the locker room, the whirlpool, a turban'd woman dries herself, applies lotion. The slit of her back-side is a gorge between snow peaks, or a dark slice of moon. She lifts one leg to the bench and a shock of black hair blooms into a rain forest. *Old women* ought to be explorers.

It's a matter of topography, I once explained to my young daughter who'd asked, "Why do painters paint naked women?" I said the body was beautiful without really believing it. She thought it was funny that I should be looking at other women, but my mother's large, shapeless body loomed over me like a white tornado; her thunderous breasts falling to her waist like boulders I was pinned under.

Philip Pearlstein maintains the languorous nudes he paints are the same to him as boulders. Some boulders, I think, as a Fellini-esque woman steps into the whirlpool. I turn my back to the jets, my body spread like a rippled table. I think of Bonnard's paintings, his wife Marthe, floating in the bathtub. She was always taking baths, suffering from a mysterious illness she pedaled from doctor to doctor; her only relief was underwater.

I don't want to get out. I feel like a shelled shrimp, pink and simple. There's a picture of Imogen Cunningham, the old photographer, and Twinka, the young model, peering at one another next to a tree, its bark crenellated like elephant skin. I remember my *bubbe* her belly, an apron over her sparse pubic hair or was that my mother? Where am I in this picture?

The Bather

after The Morning Bather by Edgar Degas, (1834-1917)

he pulls me back
inside the drawing,
my left arm swings in back
like a mannequin's,
I am easily maneuvered,
he gives me a towel,
and says, *hold steady,*
as if I were a thoroughbred,
one leg over the rim,
the other trembling,
it's cold, I tell him,
I have to blow my nose,
not yet, he says, taking a blue crayon
down my right flank,
making me look wet,
the blue scumbled stomach
rumbles,
why can't this be Manet's picnic?
foie gras and truffles,
a roll in the grass?
the line continues downward
past the towel in my hand
to the unmade bed,
dark creases in white linens,
rumpled pillow,
up to
my dark bent head.

Gaining

Her heart pounds
after the dive, still heavy
in the water. At lap
twelve, she's as thin
as a silver fish platter,
elliptical
as the sole fillet
uneaten on last night's
plate. At lap
twenty, her breasts
don't matter. She swims
not to feel her flesh—
flesh that binds
and chafes. But bones
are safe from her shark
attacks; she worships them
like relics. At lap
thirty, her shoulder blades
carve the water. At lap
sixty, she's cruising
like an arrow, bending
time and space in pool
green shadows. Past 100
she glides through
walls and doors as easily
as narrow lanes in
swimming pools, no schools
she can't be part of,
no matter
she can't penetrate.

How I Learned the Bible

"Oh, Moses, Moses," Anne Baxter moans,
wanting him to touch her, not to touch her
with his mudstained hands from the pits
for making bricks, holding her arms out
like white beguiling snakes, asking for
the length of him against her sheer
aqua gown, its liquid serendipity
accenting her sinuous hips and orchard
breasts, everything outlined for us
like in *Cliffs Notes*, especially
those precisely chiseled lips
he crushes into canned pineapple.

Stars fall a little, reconstituted
in her hair, marking how far it is
between a naked-to-the-waist Hebrew
slave, Charlton Heston, and a svelte
Egyptian princess. The air thickens
with blue intensity, the silk curtains moving
behind them like a river flowing past all
desire. Small wonder his mud doesn't
sully her, his hands molding those already
perfect shoulders. "Moses, Moses," we asked,
"how could you leave such a princess
for a piece of red slave cloth?"

True Stories

I'm going berserk, running up and down the aisles looking for a bald head decorated with one gold earring, that smug kisser. "What's the matter?" a friend shouts down the aisle. "I'm looking for Mr. Clean," I yell and we start laughing, block the aisle with our carts and howl.

Mother calls me to the television set. She wants me to see this, a dog howling "hamburger" on one of those contest shows she lives for. She believes you can get something for nothing. Married fifty years to a man who never took her anywhere, she goes on a cruise with him, pops a free seasick pill and passes out. They put her off the boat at Freeport. My father continues on to New York. He doesn't want to leave his car.

Once we had a dog named Lucky, a brown mutt my little brother adored. Every day I came home from school, I found a pool of Lucky's pee in front of my dresser and yelled. I never had an animal I loved. Lucky bit strangers at the door so my father took him away in the car.

My husband insisted on black and white tiles in our kitchen. I agreed on one condition: he'd clean it every other weekend. On Sundays he pulls the shades down, gets on his hands and knees in a white undershirt like Mr. Clean's and enjoys himself. My mother says I'm lucky.

Leda Redux

I thought I'd die, I wanted to, my eyes
rolled inside my head and my body
left me—the way the girls said. No lie—
I was never lost so completely.
I'm not what I thought, not peach fuzzed
flesh, but a pink wad of bubble, blown and burst,
I don't know how many times. I was
gone off like a string of fireworks
in the park. What came over me? A shadow
like a DC 10's wingspan or Batman's
fluttering cape, its boom-box thunder so
close overhead, my unsaddled heart ran
on its own legs to meet the driving rain.

Rouault's Daughter

Madame Bovary, c'est moi.
— *Gustave Flaubert*

Who has not been a Madame Bovary,
sold to the highest bidder, or
a sinner drunk on the purple dregs
of debauchery, plotter of serpentine
tales, thief of wiles, a murderer of picturesque
fidelity, a poisoner of the ear, simply because
of being bored when an excellent
soufflé's insensibly devoured and milky
young breasts go unsavored? Not taken
a handful only to awaken to the nightmare
of self? How could she have been so foolish
to think—to think!— that death would come
like an unlicensed plumber?

The Empty Shelves:
Berlin to Budapest by Train

You said this was going to be an easy trip. I wanted Italy—
ALONE.

*Your mother's dead just two months. I'm your husband and I
know it's not the right time for you to be alone.*

But concentration camp territory? Why not *French Highlights*
or *Barging through Burgundy*? I could hardly watch *Schlinder's
List.* (I watched it twice.) I don't even like trains.

COMPLETE AIR & RAIL VACATION.
VISIT EUROPE'S BEST-LOVED CITIES: BERLIN,
DRESDEN, PRAGUE, VIENNA AND BUDAPEST. ADMIRE
FAMOUS ARTWORK... AND ENJOY "LIFESEEING."

When did the word "train" change?
"shower"?
"camp"?

Transport. Constantly a stream of transports flowed into the
ghetto, and at many times the number of inhabitants exceeded
the normal population. People lived in continual fear of being
transported or having loved ones leave for unknown places.

"I got you out of the ghetto," my father snarls. The ghetto
of an Italian-Jewish neighborhood in Atlantic City, but what
about the ghetto of his heart? "What am I going to do after
your mother dies? At 86 I'm not interested in blow-jobs," he
rails, eyeing my plate in an overly air-conditioned restaurant in
Surfside, Florida.

Why are you crying? So the hotel room's disappointing.

Disappointing? I can't breathe. I'm crying about Mom and all the people who died here.

Your mother died from cancer, not a concentration camp.

    Elsa, blond, heavy, about 70, meets the group of 26 in front of Berlin's famous hotel "Kempi." What she must have been in her youth, saftig, hair pulled back tight, red lipstick around a torched mouth. Over the bus mic, she shouts how her mother came into the house screaming the morning after *Kristallnacht*, "All those beautiful dresses lying in the street — I love the Americans for what you did in the airlift."

    I'd like to be airlifted from this bus after driving around for two hours. The driver drops us at *Bebelplatz* to see the memorial for the book-burning: *Büchverbrennung.* I peer through glass into a hole in the ground revealing blank shelves: *The Empty Library.*

Why is This Night Different?

We never sit down like family,
we never have friends to dinner,
just Dad's relatives, Mom calls "those

bastards." On holidays, when words
like bitter herbs burn our mouths, Dad
pounds the table. No fledglings fly

from his tight fists. His blood curses,
sonuvabitch this, *sonuvabitch*
that, curdle the hot milk I'll drink

six hours later, that's how long
we have to wait not to boil a kid
in its mother's milk. When he's good

and angry he says, "Go blow it
out your ass," to Mom who's dealing
dishes like greasy playing cards.

"Trust only your own flesh and blood,"
she shouts over steaming platters
of beef *flanken*, ordering me

to taste her sweet and sour meat-
balls. Dad glares. I eat fast in case
the angel of death might not pass.

Tell me, why did I come here?

Darling, this is a long marriage. What do you think happens?

Life imprisonment. But I'm not telling it straight, bending
down to tie my shoelace in the crush of tourists snapping
pictures of the Brandenburg Gate. I remember looking down
at my old mother's paralyzed body, hands rough and red from
plucking chickens, finally smooth as a baby's, and her saying,
"It's a privilege to grow old." *Some privilege*, I thought, as her
eyes popped open and she said, "You should know where you
come from," to my daughter.

The Butcher's Daughter

My father's store smells of slaughter, hanging
sides of beef, plump gray gizzards, maroon calves'
livers. Dead chickens dress the window, dangling
like the cutouts I make with plastic scissors.
From a wrought iron hook, a cow's head's glossy
eyes follow me behind my book. A piercing

saw sears my sleep. I come downstairs, see
my mother singe a chicken by its feet; she smiles
at me in her bloodstained apron. I want
to pinch her, make her stop, but my eye catches
the cleaver in my father's hand coming down
on the block, severing lamb into chops.

The colored help, close as kin and kinder,
rescue me from the grinder. Tall George doffs
his cap, calls me *bosslady,* but it's Britty
I must mind, calling to weave my hair into plaits.
Crossing streets, Mother grabs me by the neck;
I won't hold hands that stink of chicken fat.

According to my guidebook, Hitler refused to shake Jesse
Owens' hand after he'd won four gold medals for the U.S in
the 1936 Berlin Olympics.

"Lighten up," the tour manager says, "the war didn't end
yesterday." I get up from dinner and walk back to the hotel.

Afternoon free. Perhaps
spend the time shopping
at Ka Da We or have beer
in Charlottenburg,…

Why did you scream in your sleep, "Don't leave me in Russia!"

"...kinship is one of the most primitive of tyrannies. Our real kin are those we have chosen," writes Guy Davenport.

Among the tour group, two elderly sisters, widows from Australia , white-haired and fair-skinned, Scottish origin, last of seven children speak fondly of their parents. Ann likes her scotch at tea. The others are couples, businessmen, lawyers, doctors, and housewives from the U.S. One couple has brought their precocious eight year old whose head is unusually large. The mother says, in his presence, his birth was so difficult she chose not to have more children. The child rarely seems bored, playing much of the time alone with his miniature set of Napoleon soldiers. I doubt if his head would have met Nazi standardized measurements of an Aryan.

The surroundings with so much deprivation and fear coupled with the children's natural enthusiasm and great will power intensified their cultural and creative endeavors.

Trayf

(unclean)

When I was a kid, I never sinned
in sex like my Catholic friends,
but only in what I ate,
swallowing shellfish, pig,
unkosher meats—unclean cuts,
my father said.

The first time I tasted bacon,
it was at Susan Sonnabend's.
who had a black maid,
who made it crisp and said, "Dig in."
I did, waiting for my just
punishment: death

by lightning. I walked home in wind,
rain, thunder; nothing happened.
But in case, I prayed
and promised not to smoke cigs—
Dad's Lucky Strikes or bust
into my red,

yes, piggy bank, or steal from Gersenfeld's
boardwalk sweet stand or pretend
to be more than eight,
acting the "friggin' big shot,"
my big brother said, and to trust
lies I was fed.

      After the train ride to Dresden, at yet another long
meal, the man to my right, says he's an atheist, but if
he's ever lined up against a wall, he'll be shot as a Jew.
Heidi, the guide, says Eastern Germans need to learn
to smile more. On the way to the *Grünes Gewölbe*, or
Green Vault, a treasure trove of objects with embedded
precious stones, I feel sick in traffic, jump off the bus.

Gravity

When Mother said she was going to the vault, I felt
       something wither inside, I was so young I didn't

know what a pole vault was. I didn't know gravity,
        flying to the other side of the playground escaping

countless rivals in "red rover." Knocked down again
        and again, I'd look up at the sky and imagine a dress

that pure blue color, not to cry. When does death enter
        the mind? "Give her the earrings," my father says.

"They're in the vault," my mother replies. And of course,
        now it's in a different vault from where I grew up, where

she keeps her diamond ring, pearl choker, emeralds, stuff
        I never seen her wear. Not that I care much for jewelry,

I want gems for the vault inside, not MacBeth's vaulting
        ambition, or his wife's, their bloody jewels. I want

the exalted sky Dickinson saw from her window, cathedral
        forests Lewis and Clark walked under. Closer, the vault

of my child's ski jump dreams, a half rainbow over Lake Drive,
        the arc of my husband's arm when he's away.

                                                        I put off

going to the vault to drop the new will into the safe deposit.
        When I finally went, I found insurance policies outdated,

coins from my son's collection long forgot, snapshots of art
        not worth much or already donated, the room spare

as a clean motel room with its one hard back chair and faux
        marble shelf top desk. Mother's left her jewels to the five

grandchildren, knowing I don't believe in tending plots. I leave
      everything in trust and wear my collars open.
                                                    "Give her

the ring," my father tries once more. "In the vault," my mother
          whispers, now in a hospital bed, eyes closed, head turned

to the wall. From her window on this high floor I see an opal
          beach, topaz sea, star sapphire sky, clear sparkling all.

*Be honest —you like "rooms as big as city apartments….
furnished with bright elm wood furniture…" Prague will be
better. Everyone says they love it.*

In the old Jewish cemetery in Prague, so many stones and so
crooked, "the dead live more packed than they were in life,
the stones,/packed packed./ So much love encircled!" writes
Tomas Tranströmer.

"And do you know why the synagogues, the Town Hall, the
Torahs, have all been left in place?" the staunch woman guide
asks, smiling.

And from the guidebook: *Hitler designated Prague's ghetto as
the site for the planned Exotic Museum of an Extinct Race.*

*I don't understand; why must everything come to Hitler? Can't
you appreciate the architecture or the famous people? What
about Kafka?*

His three sisters died in a camp.

Stop it! I can't take it anymore!

We pass Kepler's house, and I read aloud that in 1619 he proved planets move in ellipses, not circles, destroying a 2,000 year old belief. "Hey, did you see the figure of greed in the Old Town Hall clock *as the Jew shaking his moneybags*? That sign on that green bus?"

PRAGUE'S JEWISH QUARTER
THE GENERAL TOUR OF PRAGUE, TEREZÍN
THE "BUBBE MEISE" TOUR
AUSCHWITZ, KRAWKOW, BUDAPEST
VIENNA, BRATISLAVA, KOLÍN

Out of the 15,000 children who lived in Terezín before being deported to Auschwitz, only 100 came back. After viewing an exhibition of children's art work hanging in the Old Ceremonial Hall—"did you see that copy of a Picasso, a Vermeer, Munter?"—I hear a woman complain of the terrible tiramisù at last night's dinner.

Why do you always have to make a fuss? Why can't you let things alone?

In Vienna, Gertie, a friendly guide in her late 20s, says, "We're the only ones who could make Hitler German and Beethoven Austrian." No one laughs, but me.

In a book review a young boy says he watched the Germans tie his father's hands and then chop his beard with a blunt bayonet, wounding his face in the process. Then he went down on his knees and kissed the torturer's hands; the more he begs, the more they torment his father.

A documentary of America during the war. Hundreds of thickly bearded Orthodox rabbis outside the White House wait to see Roosevelt to protest "the events" in Europe. His schedule shows he was busy and sent someone else in his place.

Mein Kampf, Hitler says he was walking through the
alleys of Vienna when he noticed that Jews had a distinct
odor. At *Schönbrunn,* the Hapsburg summer palace,
Maria Theresa spoke to Jews only through a screen; they
were so foul to her, though much of their money built
the place. On a visit from England in 1838, the River
Wien smelled so vile to Anthony Trollope's mother that
she complained of "this black and noxious stream."

What a wife! I think you make up these things.

5 Part Invention

(1)

Her unharnessed breasts fell to her waist.
Wide red tracks rode her box-car shoulders.
Her bull's-eye nipples targeted me:
there was no escape.

(2)

Father's driving our salmon and white Olds.
He's talking to Mother next to him,
about my aunt with the lobotomy,
who forgets to wash herself: "Women
stink like fish."

(3)

Mother tries on bras and girdles. I sit
on a chair and watch her jiggle. Her belly
folds like an apron. Or is that her
mother, my old *bubbe*?

(4)

I'm dancing in the living room,
dancing like Salome, without
her seven veils, dancing for
aunts and uncles who've come
from Philadelphia, dancing
for being five. When my robe
comes opens, I'm naked as a pear.
My father's long finger quivers
in the air: will I die?

(5)

He's lying naked in August,
asleep on his bed. It's *Shabbos*,
the day of his bath. I look
the way Judith might have once,
astonished.

A sub-heading in the N.Y. Times business section reads:
Historians Are in Demand to Study Corporate Ties to Nazis.
Archivists who once wore jeans are now sporting gold cuff-
links and arriving at corporate headquarters in limousines.

This is an expensive trip. I give up.

High Maintenance

    I'm having cappuccino at a new coffee house and
I notice this woman I'm talking to has nails that are
red, squared and long, and I mean long. The first thing
I think of is are they real? She says, no, they're not.
I say why bother, and she says, low maintenance.

    I give her some poems on art I've written. She
says she's interested in reading them, but I don't
think so. She says I'm driven and she's easy, that I
write about art because I'm intellectual. I see what
she means: I hear myself say to a museum guard near
Michelangelo's last *Pietà*, "I want to touch Him, make
Him rise again." My husband says, "Are you crazy?"

    This woman is big and buxom, reminds me of my
mother and aunts when I was little. We talk about our
grown children, my son, the Donald Trump of the family;
my daughter, the new Jane Fonda of exercise videos; hers,
of course, are lazy. We talk about hair color; I'm not sure
this is going anywhere. I look at her fingers, one of them
painted with a picture of a star and moon with an embedded
rhinestone, and think of the hours and days to illuminate
a medieval manuscript, *Les Très Riches Heures*.... She
gives me the number of her cleaning lady and we leave.

    My Aunt Bea's nails were Fire Engine Red, real claws.
I haven't thought of her in years, her big tent dresses,
her clown lips matching her nails, the lipstick's smear on
her yellow teeth, toothpick in her mouth. We play gin on
the dining room table. She laughs raucously, coughing
up phlegm. "For God's sake," my father yells, "quit
smoking, you goddamn cow, or you'll kill yourself."

I've never been to where she lives. Her ex-husband comes into my father's store and curses our family. Everybody in our family is always angry. Her son, Sammy, with the acne, curses the family and goes into the army. Aunt Bea dies of a stroke after I move away. I get to read her records in the high school office. All A's. Her and me.

My son and I are in the same place as I was with the woman with the artificial nails, having coffee. I'm filling his plate with breads and cakes as he's telling me he's got to get rid of his girlfriend, "high maintenance." "Expensive dates?" I ask, tearing into fresh sourdough. "No," he says, "it takes her an hour to shower and dress. I want someone ready just like that."

"How's your crazy aunt?" a rich girlfriend's mother asks, "you know, the one with the lobotomy?" Knocking the bottom out of me. Turns out my father signed the papers. They wouldn't put her in a home and she needed care, more than we could give.

But he didn't sign the papers; your grandmother did.

Yes, but it feels truthful.

In a Viennese coffee shop I meet a woman from Dallas who's singing in a choir traveling through Europe. They're supposed to appear in Budapest next. But when I go, I read a sign saying the concert's canceled. Inside I arrive in time for the *Mourner's Prayer*, the *Kaddish*, and stand to recite it with a few others. The synagogue is almost empty. As a child, I felt embarrassed for the mourners; I don't know why. Look at that—two balconies leading up to the dome. Every time the child recites the prayer, the parent's soul rises higher in Heaven.

34

Things I Don't Know

My head presses against the wood rail
      between the brass rings of the velvet curtain,
            screening the women from the men below.

It's *Rosh Hoshanah,* the New Year, and my
      new wool clothes itch in the warm synagogue
            as pear yellow light in each small alcove

of the balcony floats down to where my father,
      in a clean shirt and dark suit, kisses the fringes
            of his prayer shawl as he rocks back and forth.

My older brother does what my father does,
      a few seconds behind him. The baby of the family,
            three, sits on a bench, swaying his legs.

My father looks up and smiles—his half-smile,
      as if he's counting on me, but I don't know for what.
            Mother doesn't see because she's talking

recipes with the dry cleaner's wife. Across the balcony,
      the *bubbes,* sallow with moles and mustaches, *davan*
            like the men below. They stand at the rail,

dabbing their eyes under their glasses with hankies,
      blowing their noses, hard. Mother says, "two eggs"
            when I ask, "Why are the *bubbes* crying?"

It's *Rosh Hoshanah* and I have new clothes.

Let's change the subject. You like the baths.

The Géllert Hotel is nice. But when I see all those naked bodies— . In a magazine *Luxury Islands*, I read what a New Jersey plumber saw at Margaret Island—*Margitsziget,* famous for its thermal treatments: "I was fourteen. We lived in Buda. I saw the Germans line the Jewish people up on the quay. Then they shot them. The bodies fell in the river. My blue Danube turned red. It was terrible. Why would anyone want to do something like that?"

Atlantic City, 1950/1999

Was it the rub of cool clammy sand
                on my small feet, or slippery
        moss-covered rocks by pier

pilings that made me afraid to walk under
                needles of light? Along the edge
        of an autumn beach near

the end of a boardwalk I never thought
                ended anywhere, I wept
        before throwing dirt over

a box by a double headstone. Beloved
                and beloved, they followed each
        other like evening

swallows, their tracks on the beach covered
                with other tracks. Sunlight breaks
        on an incoming

wave that crests like the plumage of some wild
                bird. Once I fled from squealing
        bomber seagulls over

the hard-packed sand, zigzagged like herring
                bone gold bracelets. Late morning
        hinged to a pink horizon, white

frill of the sea slides decorously up the leg
                of the beach where Mother, copper-
        toned and busty, in a green

and white chair, with a bag of fruit, anchors
            a breezy circle of ladies, my
        torso bare, like the smaller

child in Sorolla's painting of two sisters
            holding hands in the shallows,
        tawny shadows pooling

at their feet. How many crabs did I set
            on their backs? No sister,—
        drifting like an empty bottle.

Part Two

In the Musée d'Orsay

I know this is paradise . . .
　　　—Philip Larkin

When I saw them I knew right away
What they were like in bed,
Their lithe bodies fucking into
Heaven, both of them zipped up
In leather, her tall languid body
Leaning on his willowy frame—
Pasty skinned. As they looked
At the pictures, they were the picture
Of everything I'd not been.

I used to dream of that unlived life,
Rampant with rage I'd let it go by
Until I became a middle-aged wife,
And everyone who'd been my age joined me,

Kissing off that kind of happiness. I'd wonder
At the lost opportunities and what if . . . .
But why didn't I? It wasn't about God

Or getting pregnant or even whispers—of what?
What stopped me from going to hell was
My will not to be taken, and now,
Stricken with sadness at the thought of this couple,
I wander through the museum under its pouring skylights,
And beyond, the noises of the street traffic, with the light
　　　　cumulous clouds, *fair weather*
Clouds streaming endlessly overhead.

Pity

She wanted to die, but she also wanted to live in Paris.
—*Gustave Flaubert*

I've had those days, when
melancholia is true
blue, faithful

as a three-legged
dog asleep at the hearth,
and you can't

shake the shag rug hard
to make the blues fly like
notes, and you

cry until you're broke
like a Sèvres plate
someone drops

from Louis' table. Picture
plump Fragonard
from Grasse, lush

flower-filled, famous
for its perfume, even
a sheep's white

dreadlocks smell of dew
beside a hapless chic
shepherdess —

Marie Antoinette—playing,
then plea-
bargaining

for her head before
it rolls. Poor rosy-cheeked
Fragonard

who lost everything
after the revolution.
Pity Madame

Bovary who never
saw Paris or walked a three-
legged dog.

The Other Side

I hate Monet. I hate the cathedrals
that melt like ice cream cones in front of you
and drip on all your clothes. I hate a hard
sky's obstinacy; I lack faith
in all that crusty scaffolding.
Didn't he want to see
the other side of Naples' bay?

I don't want my riverbanks looking
for Narcissus.
I want a looking glass that sees.
I want apples with a hard circumference,
not succotash in my mouth.
I want my Poles spelled out.

I don't want my flowers flirting,
flitting cigarette ashes in my parlor,
and I don't want my houses to rise
and fall with the weather.
I don't want to drown my friends
in endless streams of light.
I want to see people waking
into their outlines,
throw off the shades of night.
If I had a wife to dream of
like Camille, I wouldn't paint veils
like fortress walls around her.

I'd let my garden grow
wild and leave my easels planted
near window sills and catch
the sunlight in my mouth.
I wouldn't dust a single leaf,
clip a drooping frond.
If I didn't like the perfume
of dead flowers, I wouldn't
plant seeds of joy.

Joan Confesses

The best part, by far, was hearing the voices,
and then I suppose having my hair cut,
(not a great loss since I lacked the feminine
art to make much from little), and of course,
riding a horse in rough pants, for which
I paid with my heart. The judges said I'd sinned
against God by my clothes. For that my naked soul
flew like an arrow from the flames. I won't speak
about the pain; I had many enemies.
But of the voices and the light and the sound
of the bells floating through me, until
my soul dappled in shades of pearl gray, spiraled . . . .
Some silly girls say they saw my feet leave
the ground in a race on the hilltop.
God knows I wanted to go home after
my gentle dauphin was crowned. Yes,
to spinning and peeling potatoes, tending the sheep,
but it wasn't for me to choose. The voices said
I must be good; I could not leave until
France was saved. How did I know they were angels?
How did I know my mother and father?
When I heard the harp's sweet notes at court,
I smiled. They were wrong to call it heavenly
music. Yes, I'd do it again, as a man.

Mutton

". . . but no one ever painted a female
Sebastian, did they?"
  —*T.S. Eliot*

I wonder what St. Sebastian ate
for dinner? Pierced with arrows, he swoons,
rolls his brown eyes upward, then down
to see the blood dripping from his horrific
wounds. Blood in thin calligraphic lines,
handwriting as clear as the handwriting
on the wall —*Number, Numbers, Scales* . . . .
Do I dare take another chocolate truffle
or macaroon? His muscled arms, bound
and smooth, his slender ankles tied
like Andromeda's. I'd like to undo him,
give him a Reese's peanut butter cup.

What do we do for love or is it
self-love? Offer the chalice of the body
to the surgeon? Wait in line to receive
the telltale signs of a tummy tuck or breast
augmentation? Note the arrow penetrating
the young man through the taut neck, out
the unplowed forehead. Everything
carved and hard on him, even the loincloth,
the marmoreal body arched

                    as mine is
on the cosmetologist's table waiting
for her to rip off the tape, pulling up
the hair. But first came the hot honey-
almond wax, when I was unable to stifle
a shudder, the skin, soft and tender,
where hip meets leg like a nice joint
of mutton. Why do I want to be a female
Sebastian? By his pedestal lies a foot
on the neck of a broken woman.

Wild Beasts

after Conversation, Henri Matisse (1869-1973)

(1)

This isn't about his favorite pair of striped pajamas
she failed to sew a button on or her closed dressing
gown, black as a panther like her mood, but the space
between them where "non" is written in the grillwork
of the open window. Her will be done . . . .

(2)

He stands, imposing his silence on her, like you do
when you're angry and twitch your fingers and thumbs in
your pockets, while I sit on a throne, barely sketched in
there, like she does, unforgiving as stone, laying down the
law, each of us locked outside that pink bordered garden.

(3)

Amélie made hats to support them, farmed out
the kids to relatives. Now she wants his interest, but this
conversation isn't going anywhere. It's his only painting of
two people facing each other. Why didn't you say something?
I thought silence was a weakness until I saw Henri and

followed Amélie's black sleeve to the window's curlicue
"non." The blue void on the other side connects Henri to
Henri. I wanted to find the crack in you. Henri is hard.
Amélie fights back. Why do we think they're arguing about
another woman? Because he's the one behind bars.

(5)

Is bliss always outside? She was everything to him.
What's missing between them? They're growling from
hunger. He can't change his stripes. But they're not us.
Ask me for something: French toast, coffee, the good
married life. Lie down with me. We can die from want.

Michelangelo's Last Pietà

after Pietà Rondanini, Michelangelo Buonarroti (1475-1564)

                    I wonder
what took Michelangelo so long
to bring Mary to age.
Here, the other women wrinkle like dates.
Parchment tongues writing
in flames. Gladiators and that sort
of thing.
I thought it was a
miracle. A bald faced
lie. She had other
children, but eyes only for

Him,
with the body of a pagan
god. I want to touch
His legs, still beautiful,
I want to touch
him as Michelangelo did,
behind the favored ear, under
riddled testicles, make him
laugh again,
my rolled tongue to Gorgon's
invisible navel—
o, closed pigeon-eye,
cool dove, come as I listen
as she did, and kiss him
wherever
there is no blood.

Picasso's Canon

I could not bear to be loved by Picasso
who grinds and churns a woman's body
into fodder for the Minotaur's ego.
He wields shapely Fernande into a squat
brown native and inflates Marie Thérèse
into a blowsy beachball bather. (Her nose
swells into a penis.) For each new mistress,
he's full of *tendresse* but then he grows
into a galloping sadist. He marries
Olga thinking he wants a proper wife.
Diaghilev's Russian ballerina carries
herself so-so on toes, but falls in the strife.
Giant Madonna or monster with claws,
she's tied to an armchair with toothy jaws.

I could not bear to be loved by Picasso,
bent into a weeping martyr like Dora
Maar for the sake of his art. He blows
her off when Gilot enters the corrida.
This *femme-fleur* tries not to lower her guard,
for she'll bleed like a cut stalk. On canvas
and in bed, his women overlap. Hard-
headed and smart, she leaves him aghast
with this parting shot: "Picasso eats
art." No matter how much he loves, this frog-
prince portrays his women as baiting beasts,
each orifice a mouth seeking his cod-
piece. Bowed Jacqueline calls him *Monseigneur.*
In time, he paints her peeing on the floor.

Beast

"I am the one sir, that comes to tell
you your daughter and the moor are
making the beast with two backs . . ."
    —Shakespeare, Othello (I, 1, 117)

I know that beast without
a face, its swan's snowdown
neck, black bull's head, snake-
skin's press, cow's sour cud
breath, wolf's eye-teeth, stag
swaggering antlers, a rocking
Trojan horse without brakes,
it sucks like Charybdis,
expels like a whale or stands
impaled—Our Lady's unicorn
uncorraled, its limbs wrap
like bands on a Christmas
box, the ox and ass no less
a part of that dumb scene
than bearded gift-bearing
kings. I've heard that beast
sing a cappella off key, grunt
like a pig at the trough,
low like a cow being led
unwillingly. I've heard it
cry out names, yours and mine—
mostly. I've smelled that beast's
hot and heavy perfume, felt
its cool shaven surfaces,
nestled inside its furry
demesne, borrowed its blind
Samson strength, let it
crush me, take me
to the terrible limit.

Adios, Caravaggio

I'm sick of blood spurting
like ruby silk strings
you cut loose from the heads
of monsters: Goliath,
Medusa—your own
snake pit. I can still
hear the child scream
to Abraham. I'm sick,
too, of your bloated
virgin pulled from
the Tiber like
a drunken
hooker, all those old men's spindly
ribs, hearts feeble
as canaries, old
women's harrowing,
incised faces, your sleight
of hand more deft
than your spiffy
cardsharps', your boys' limp
pricks, echoing soft arc
of birdwing, the young,
voluptuous flesh cradled
by the dumb, breathing
animal. How the light
shines equally on the arm
of the muscled, dark-
haired executioner, and the still
pulsing breast of Salome,
on the serene,
severed head of the Baptist,
shiny fat globules on the cleaver.
I can't shake my eyes.

54

La Mort et Orphée

after Jean Cocteau's Orphée

(1)

No wonder Orphée falls in love with Princess
Death, her seal black hair pulled into a perfect widow's
peak reveals a flawless mask, her hour-glass points
to a beachhead at Normandy. She could strut down
a runway in an old Dior and nobody would see

(2)

time running out. No one hears Death cutting through
mirrors. She stands over Orphée's and Eurydice's twin beds,
thinking how to get rid of her. When she hugs him and says,
"You still have a human warmth," I feel sorry for her.

(3)

His wife rides away on her bicycle— because
he's impossible— like a husband tinkering with his
car forever. Orphée jots down stock market reports
and oracles from a dead poet over the car radio. Why
does Death seem so alive, he's electrified by a fire

(4)

that burns like ice? Pulled by Princess Death, an invisible
tango artist, Orphée drags his feet going after Eurydice.
Death wants him badly, but something in him wants to live in
the room upstairs overlooking the fields, between line-

dried sheets, creamy thighs. Is Death kind returning them to life? How long before the vine snaps? The baby's colic, an affair with a barmaid, or worse—war? How long before he wants to wear the black velvet gloves of Princess Death?

An Ordinary Day

Early sunlight, and a white
nightgowned wife's watering
the grass—not her usual

task, but her mate's away
at a fortieth high school
reunion. A fool,

she expects, seeing him
with an old flame, standing
around lonely-like

at the cash bar, wishing
for a moment he'd married
her. Not wanting to go,

the wife stayed home
to be on her own,
to test the waters,

seeing sprinklers
arc's spray have
a scope that women

are incapable of,
according to Freud, or so
says Camille Paglia,

"Freud thinks primitive
man preened himself
on his ability

to put out a fire
with a stream of
urine. A strange thing

to be proud of but
certainly beyond
the scope of women."

A strange thing,
indeed, the neighbors
think, her getting wet

like that, calling out
to her, " how are you,"
"how are you."

"Good, good," she replies,
hearing herself say,
"liar, liar."

Waitressing

When everyone leaves the house,
I breath easier
(with Tchaikovsky
in the background),
picking up coffee mugs
and plates of toasted crumbs
with orange marmalade,
I hear *Capriccio Italien*
and I am
on the Piazza San Marco
picking up after patrons
at the Caffé Florian;
the light is hazy,
soft and warm and sealaden;
the umbrellas are folded
at tables nearly empty;
a German tourist shuts his eyes
and drums his fingers,
dreaming of California
beaches.

Alberto Giacometti's Wife

Large Seated Woman, 1958-59

I cannot keep my hands
from running over the gouges,
the cracks, the slashes
in her rigid body,
tracing the pocketknife's
transverse through her chest
to feel what he did,
working her over
night after night
under a burning light bulb.

My hands become nimble following his,
clay covered and caked,
kneading her shoulders,
neck, molding
the downcast breasts,
the hollow of her lap,
searching for her waist.
For him, there is no resting place.
He cannot finish her off.

She gave herself to art, too —
wanting to be his wife.
She was always wanting
this or that,
but mostly indoor plumbing.
That would make her happy.
Herr Macher,
he would fix her —
with hands like stumps, embedded
in her body.
The price of art? —
ask Mrs. Giacometti.

That Bitch-Goddess

*So then, when you'd got your hands on the
girl, did you take turns at balling her,
seeing that she liked swapping husbands?*
    —Euripides

You weren't carried off on Paris' back like the blond,
        blue-eyed babe in Gozzoli's *The Rape of Helen*, looking

wistfully back at a house full of guests. Good looks attract
        good looks and you were taken with Paris' curly locks,

golden Oriental robes. Paris was ambrosia after a steady
        diet of Spartan fish and lamb. And yet you said of

Aphrodite, it was that bitch who caused you to leave your
        husband's bed for twenty years. Even you admitted

Menelaus wasn't short on brains or fine body parts. So why
        blame good looks for your unhappiness? I look

between the covers of fashion magazines and see women
        standing, looking mean, reaching their hands into

tight jeans. "Princess, pearl of kings," what was it like
        to pass from a stately king to a young prince, then to

his brother, before Menelaus fetched you? How fast you were
        to forget how sweet your husband was just after

Hermione came, *she was only a girl*, feeding your ravenous,
        but small, pink mouth, black grapes and honeyed

treats. The women in the magazines have their hair whipped
        by wind or slicked by gel; their otherwise depilated

bodies shine off the page. Tall in your long gown, in your
       silver cloak, "enticing Helen," what did you feel

when middle-age crept over your liquid ramparts, when a
       little belly shook as you walked? Did you agonize

that Paris might run around, looking for a younger crowd,
       did you want him to, tiring of his perfumed skin,

banal compliments? Then would you imagine Menelaus' fair-
       haired body against your still lithe limbs? The women

in the fashion ads will grow old, too, but not in public
       view. Enfolded in a shining robe, hoping beauty

would save you, and it did, Helen, thinking of your own skin,
       you did what any mortal would do: you covered your

pearly ass. You said it was a phantom who went with Paris
       while you stayed in Egypt and took hot baths. *All*

women are not Helen . . . but have Helen in their hearts. I look
       for you in the ads, on the movie screen, in dressing

room mirrors. How often it takes a Paris and a beauty
       contest to make Eros surface on a dolphin's back.

Downsizing

She had the whole lake
for a view, but then
they moved, now it's just

a hole through someone
else's window. She
gave it up, wanting

something new between
them. The onset of
winter staring them

straight in the bull's eye,
this quiet man
and his nagging wife.

*Change your tie, lose some
weight, get rid of those
raggy undershirts.*

And then she couldn't
remember him young
anymore. All white

bearded and furry
chested, fur-bellied,
he lay in bed like

a parked whale—faithful
for life, aren't they?
If only he would

say something new. *Look,*
rain. A full moon. Geese
overhead. But what's

left after ripeness
is often a point
of view, like his when

he imagines her nude
on the staircase, having
fallen and broken

her neck. Was that it?
Was it, *was it* os-
teoporosis—

no, he pushed her down
a flight of stairs. *Pain*
in the ass, he says,

looking out over a flat
roof across the street
where he can barely

make out, just barely,
between two houses,
a band of deep blue,

the lake she loved. Why,
she should save him
the trouble and drown.

The Great Canopy

Full blown trees converged as the driver
slumped over the wheel and the car swerved,
heading for the lone patch of grass
between neighbors, the impact with chimney
killing the teen instantly.   How is the street
to understand it was responsible? Amid
the framed beauty of houses dark
and safely locked, inhabitants asleep
at 2 a.m., the drunken boy
drove deeper into despair, barred
from this palatial ease. How
the openness of the tree-lined avenue bore down
like a great canopy. No way out
for him but through my living room.

Housewife

When did I
become its clanging ducts and
banging shutters, broken

green roof tiles and rusted out
gutters? Where are the polished
oak staircases, the white

vaulted ceilings? Instead I
saw nine bricks crumble while
rain soaked walls dissolved

into webbed stains. Spiders
wept while I began to slip
from my cracked

foundation. I dreamt
the basement caved, the house
became a grave,

a Piranesi ruin I roamed
like a hermit watching
weeds like cataracts climb

the sunroom blocking
my view of the lake
and bluff. What made me

give it up? Dank and dark
the house withdrew
its charms. I traipsed

stairwells clobbering
mice before hammering
a "for sale" sign

in the ground while my
lobotomized aunt, shamefully
rouged and fat, wagging

her red-nailed talon, predicts,
*you'll be sorry, you're no good
and never will be.*

Vuillard's Mantelpiece

"I've never been anything but a spectator."
—Edouard Vuillard (1868-1940)

    The corseted widow in crisp black, Venus on the
mantel in a light coat of dust, Maman bending before
her, lighting the stove, stoking it, "Maman is my muse,"
he told everyone, she is the breadwinner: cut and stitch,
thread and rip, corsets spring undone, hook together in
their small apartment. The son watches, keeps in his head
smells of sachet, pressed young or old goose wrinkled flesh,
swish of satin, sizzle of iron, hissing tea kettle's rising steam
clouds, an impatient Venus looking out from a curtain, and
sees the pattern changing and unchanging like the sea she
rose from, her navel eye surfacing higher than the Tanagra
figures or Maillol models, higher than the Degas ballerina
fixing her pink hair ribbon before a much reduced Antinous
cast in shadow. Venus, a true goddess, looks beyond the
brooms in the corner, turned up corners of carpets, stacks of
unfinished pictures, leftover biscuits. Her turned pelvis, sloped
shoulders, cutoff arms, what we call classical charms, tame
the domestic wilderness, for us, for the bachelor Vuillard.

The Fifth Wonder of the World

*In her most majestic shrine, . . . the worshiper could
see, placed on a votive table, an image of Hera's
mouth closing amorously around Zeus' erect phallus.*
    —Roberto Calasso in The Marriage of Cadmus and Harmony

Now that my beard is full and hoary,
a horny, goatish god . . . you're thinking
who'd have me unless I changed into
a gorgeous hunk of white bull or softest
swan. You've got it wrong. About Hera
and me. I chased women, a few boys.
Not because she was a harpy, a bitch,
a gadfly. She was a delight — after all,
she schooled me, this loveliest of sisters.
We petted for three hundred years.
The bed is her place *par excellence*.
It was hard getting her out of it.
Hera, of the white arms, took me as if
she were sucking up a strawberry soda.
But marriage is a different ballgame. And
Hera knew it. I came to her as a half-frozen
cuckoo, pecked in her lap. Who can resist
the cooing of a soft bird until it grows
hard between her hands? By then, it's too late.
What's in the word wife that causes men
to close their eyes, freezes up the iron supply?
Gods don't have blood, but we imagine it.
I saw how mortal women shivered and came
near faint. A goddess goes on and on
indefinitely. Lights on or off, it's monogamy.
Hera was hoodwinked. Who hasn't wanted
to change skins, try out a pair of wings,
rain down in a shower of gold, slither

inside a serpent to get around? Hera,
my wife, my sister, my other, forgot
I was quintessentially a lover
before a husband. They leave out that part.

Desire

Once I wanted a Hermès scarf
like the girls wear on the beach
at Deauville, you know how
those ads make you want to be bad,
the girls with their long hair
blowing, their Brigitte Bardot mouths
open for invisible hooks,
their unblemished legs spread.

At Neiman-Marcus I spread out
the scarf, four winged seahorses
and four golden gondolas drift
in a brilliant blue lagoon.
This is art. The lion of St. Mark
grimaces like Bert Lahr. I, too,
met a wizard who trafficked
in medals and false hearts.

Once I wanted a husband who'd shape
my life like Dr. Diver in *Tender
is the Night*. I wanted pearls
like his wife's, as much as the starlet
Rosemary wants her husband,
who wants back his life.
By the time I finished,
I wanted the whole goddamn Riviera.

By then I was a wife
like Lucretia in Tintoretto's
painting. Her pearls fall one by one
as she falls to Tarquin.
Their fleshy bodies tumble out of
the canvas. The pearls roll on the floor
like blank dice. All but one. Caught
in the diaphanous cloth uncovering her.
I   want   to   stop   that   pearl.

The Movie Version

Why do I scare when she jumps
into the shoes and their slippery ribbons wrap
around her legs like red metallic snakes? From
top to bottom, she's aflame, stuck fast, until
she throws herself off the balcony onto
a moving train, torn between the dance and
a husband. What is it with her and Anna K.—
rushing to caterwauling trains like lovers?
What do I want? What do I want in the store

window? Do I dare put on the red shoes
that glow like flaming gladioli, carved by
a diabolic cobbler for Moira Shearer
in the movie version? Her hair's so red,
it looks cartoonish. The shoes beckon,
radiating neon circles, drawing me
to the fire. They don't even have to be red
ballet slippers; black pumps or supple suede
boots with zip-off colored panels can woo
just as well. This thing about putting my foot
into destiny like Cinderella, Dorothy —
if it fits, I win a husband or magical
properties:

I spin like Pavlova,
wear a tuxedo like Dietrich, have hair
like Harlow, skin like Garbo; my face fills
the screen like a fresh gardenia; my silhouette
rises with an upraised fist. I burn the reel.

74

Raw

As in a shucked
oyster, the pearl
lying replete
in its nacreous
bed, or a cold fiery
star streaming
utter from its pitch
continent between moon
horns, or a dewdrop
hugging pure the husk of morning
corn, each in its cardinal
realm: the calm
pond of your rippling
smile, the autumn orchard
of your unforgivable
dark crop, the pale
beach of your undulating
back, the crystal
clear of your candle,
kindling my raw
feet. Such wanting has its own
breath — such wanting
is merciless.

Deluge

Without the crooked
furrow splicing my
forehead's strained

center, filigree
of red spidering, indigo
rivers, blue marble

branches, the fine
rivulets and deep
laid fishnets, the body's

exposed
calligraphy, without
the cross-

hatching of hardened
incisions, the fallen
and slightly disappointed

scallop of mother
breasts, the surgeon's purple
X targeting

nosegay nipple, without
the pulsing soft white
belly's stretched

ribbons fading
into my navel's blue valley,
disappeared of birth

and sunlight, but I
would not come
to you without

the births and deaths
of all the beloveds,
how else?

Monet's Liquid Walls

Cathedrals melt before your gaze,
skies jell into oceans, ice floes
break up, move faster down the Seine.

People step out of their outlines
to bathe in your endless streams
of day. Where is the ground beneath

your feet or are you always floating
in *la mer*? Dutch houses glisten:
gray pearls in your unborn world.

For you, nasturtiums dance a slow
blue ballet and sunflowers flirt,
flitting golden lashes. Poplar

trees find their twins in upside down
gardens and riverbanks fall in.
The earth doubles and loses itself

in quivering ponds. As Camille,
the wife you loved lies on her bed,
you watch death paint her hardening

face, noting all the slow moving
shades: soft violet turning yellow
to cold gray. You forget your place.

Later you paint her like Ophelia,
a bride under a veil of drifting
white threads, drifting further away.

No dust rests on your lilypads.
Dead flowerheads vanish before
you arrive. What you once saw and

let go, you entrap in a thick
net of paint. But how not to kill
a thing and keep it? You hate black,

drive it from your palette. But it
creeps into your stern speech: your black,
black days. You try to dissolve it

in coastal mists, morning scenes, smoke-
stacks in London, silk Venetian
fog, filling in the living light

between things, building liquid walls.
At night when I lie awake next
to my sleeping husband, whose back

I ache to touch, I think of your
dissolving in this world, and what
I could do with your velvet brush.

Part Three

The Change

    I am the silver in my hair, the lightning released in whitecaps rushing below the footpath along the bay, I am the shore on the other side, curving and indolent, the red-in- the-wings of a blackbird shooting through my eye, I am the twig fingers, water and sky pour through day and night, the golden eyes of dandelions, common and generous, the empty bench looking out to sea, the brown paper lunch bag curled by the tree, I am the last wedded leaves and the falling yellow faithless, the tough needles of an evergreen sentry, my boots' honest brown laces, the reel pulling in schools of mackerel skies swimming over blue horizons, flooding houses at dinnertime with unpredictable weather, "What's for supper, Mom?" I hear my old teenage voice resound, "I hate fish," and the words fly back, stream out again, "I loved it all, Mom," I leave that house and pass into the people I pass, the black aide holding an elderly man's white arm, he is so white, he's almost a cloud; she is so wide, her hips block, I pass and soar to the clouds, hiding the belly of the shadow I shed on the beaten grass, breeding grounds for the apple I toss, core of empires blossoming in my head, I am the eye that stares back from the cement, the breadth of pyramids, bent horizons, horned moons, my legs flying ahead of me, carried by Nikes, Pegasus, Icarus, Athena, I am leaving my outlines indefinite, look for me, I loved you.

The Prevailing Angel

after Jacob and the Angel, Jacob Epstein (1880-1959)

Hovering like a rain
cloud, a thunder-
clap, then the stranger's
mighty arms drawing
him in, the massive

hands hugging the sharp
shoulder blades, Jacob
limp before the wind-
swept locks of this rapturous

angel, his own damp curls
cropped, heavy arms
stupefied. The man-angel
squats to take in Jacob's
strong member between
his fortress thighs.

Years later, lying
with his hard-won bride, Rachael,
their sinewy legs entwined
as the knurled vines
of their ancestors, Jacob
presses open the sky, looking
for the angel.

Man After His Bath

And when I saw you climbing out of your
bath, I knew I hadn't made a mistake—your body
as you turned and twisted a towel, no longer
white, and draped it around your thicker waist,
your back turned like a desert god's, Charlton
Heston as Moses, stripped to the waist, holding
an Egyptian princess in his arms, those muscled
arms. I'm going back to the time when I scotchtaped
pictures of movie stars on the eave above
my bed in a small Cape Cod in Margate, NJ,
a block from the ocean Burt Lancaster
and Deborah Kerr lay for eternity,
the tide sweeping them, and Jennifer Jones
waited on a hilltop for William Holden
to come back from Korea, or *The World
of Suzie Wong*. But perhaps, I had it wrong—
the largeness of their dream, their indefinite
yearning. It's what we touch with our hands
that makes us lonely, though something of the stars
lingers, and we want it again, your white head
bent as you raised a sculpted leg to the bench,
tending to your feet, so clean and neat
after all these years, thinking how I wish
we could meet in the garden where you are first
among men, and I'm not a snake.

Almost A Love Poem

You are my refuge and my home, my husband.
    —Penelope in Ovid's Heroides

I don't know how to write a love poem, I unravel them
    in my sleep beside you, waking with dread you

might not be here. Married as many years as Penelope
    missed Ulysses' muscled body, I imagine "hazards

more awful than real." I travel the map of your face, my
    finger tracing the wide bridge of your noble nose,

your high forehead, rising every year, your hair thinning
    to a few unruly silver reeds. In the fifth grade

I remember Mrs. McGeary, her tight skirts and spike heels,
    her forehead smeared with ashes, sat on her desk

before the class, one leg crossed over the other and told
    us the dead will rise on Judgment Day, but this

was Ash Wednesday, 1955.   I saw skeletons overturn
    headstones, wave their bones in jubilation. Later,

when I went up to her desk for more paper, I saw her writing
    a letter to her husband, a major in the Air Force

in Korea, "My darling, come home safe." When my grandmother
    died later that year, my father cried in the kitchen

all night. I know because I slept downstairs in my parents'
    pushed together twin beds, with the door open, afraid

of the dark closing me in. In the morning I told my father
    not to cry because the dead rise. Shaking my shoulders

he said, "Since when do you believe in Jesus Christ?" We
        were Jewish; I didn't know, but I guessed right.

The first cold Sunday in October, gossamer columns of
        sunlight break through the low cloud cover, the kind

of day we walk in the park late afternoon and I point
        to "Jesus beams," that unearthly light that comes in

old movies after crucifixions or Christians are fed to the lions:
        Quo Vadis, The Robe, Spartacus. I loved those movies;

I have always wanted to believe always in the resurrection of the
        body. My darling, we sleep back to belly, I fill

the curve of your wide, ample bowl. That's what frightened
        Penelope the most, I think, sleeping alone on the edge

of a world. We stood under the *huppa,* the white flowing
        canopy — you know what Sholom Aleichem said?

"You enter it living and come out a corpse."

Naked Companions

after Matisse's Luxe, calme, et volupté (1904-1905)

Was the painting for his wife Amélie,
the one sitting erect, gritting her teeth?

Her wide skirts spread on the beach like a ship's
blue sails, beside her naked companions,

five women and a young girl, gathered
for tea. At her feet lies a white cloth set

with china cups and saucers. Broken water
and land shimmer with red heat. Their flesh

dissolves into specks of ripe color, water-
melon's melodious greens, peach's bold

rouge, grape's lush violets—all but Amélie's.
Compact as a Menton lemon, she's thinking

of tea. Barely an outline holds them
together, only the grip of Henri Matisse.

Why does he call them this hot afternoon
at the beach? What invitation is dropped

through the slot? The girl wonders why she's
included among the wild beasts; she stares

at their breasts and buttocks. Who looks at
the woman with her back turned behind Amélie,

her arms outstretched like Christ's? Is she
the enemy? What can't he get from his wife

that he gets from the others, the ones
lying down, brushing starfish from salt-knotted

strands, the ones who crawled out of the sea?
Why does he want them to meet? The mother,

the sister, the lover, the child. Perhaps
we can never have the whole person.

The Cunning of Edgar Degas

Edgar Degar (1834-1917)

They say I don't like women, that I make
them ugly. Women washing their private parts,
like cats licking themselves clean, they find
indecent. *Why do I?* they ask. Even my ballerinas
fail to escape the public's wrath. They say
I draw as if I were staring through a keyhole.
I don't have to. Prostitutes, dancers, laundresses,
give me entrance freely. Neither handsome
nor charming, I come and go like a doctor
making a house call. "Draw lines, young man,"
Ingres said, "and you will be a good artist."
I take my crayon everywhere, (not *en plein air*,
that's for anglers!) to the opera, brothel, milliner,
making myself most disagreeable, moving an arm
or leg, to get the right angle. Impressionist?
Don't be ridiculous! It's back to the studio for hours,
months, years, for the product's never finished.
Again ask, *why do I?*

I watched my Creole mother's beauty wilt
like hothouse gardenia's. She died
when I was thirteen; puberty spilled into
a grave. I had aunts, sisters. Just the same
the approach to women grew formidable.
Still, the heart craves the natural, if not
the flesh. A simple task like brushing the hair
of an animal becomes an act of tenderness.
Did I hate women? Say I hated horses then.
See her squatting in the tub, the thick flesh forms
into ancient folds; hear the water trickling
under her breasts, armpits, between her legs.

Mysterious darkness! I drew it all, except
for the smell as the critics claimed. (When paint
and canvas failed, I tried poetry.) Behind
the scenes at the opera, the dancers reined in,
like horses at Anges before a race, eager
and tense, I breathed in their sweat. I learned
the names of the steps, even the strokes
of the laundress. They pressed on my brain
like a fever. Their pain, my *joie de vivre*.

O'Keeffe's Black Door

I bought the place because it had that door in the patio. I had no peace until I bought the house. I'm always trying to paint that door—I never quite get it.
—Georgia O'Keeffe

It is harder to get that black space in the door
than to pass through the eye of a black iris
or to sleep in a black place splintered by lightning,
it is easier to climb the twisted strands of D. H. Lawrence's
tree than to believe they're pubic hairs, it is easier
to fly with the crows over Lake George, soar with a black
bird over snow-covered peaks, it is easier, it is easier
to hold out your arms like a black cross blessing
red and yellow ribbons of dying sunlight
than to put one foot in that black door.

Who would believe there's so much black in O'Keeffe,
black to offset the sleeping white pearl between
bone strips of sloping thighs, carved
from the moon's roving eye shadow, the pearl
generating a roulette wheel of a black bull's-eye,
the black iridescence removed from the bride,
the gem residue from the black strips of a closed
clamshell, all we know of night and dark angels.

It is harder to get to that black space in the door
than to be a black pear with a mouth, to be inside
the black of a red poppy and not be blinded
by raw perfume. Easier to come back down a black
winter road or go wandering off the canvas, easier
to be a widening V, a white shaft opening
like a cervix or the white in the jack-in-the-
pulpit, going up into the blue-black velvet—

Mammogram

My bleating breast pressed like a veal patty
for the x-ray wants to lie down in a green pasture
and be comforted by babbling waters trickling
near a homestead, wants to chew the cud, nuzzle
the nipple mouth in the earth, suck the sunlight
and the rain. It wants to nose around
a flower's petals and get stiff in love, squirt
copiously like a child's water pistol, dream of
native sisters, brown berried, bobbing in the open.

In the waiting room we sit in the same robes,
members of an order, waiting to be inscribed
into a Book of Life, heads down in *G.Q.*'s trousers,
Architectural Digest's treasure houses, *Gourmet's*
whipped trifles, *Vogue's* fantasy emporiums.
Not all the advertisements of Chanel can dispel
this rancid anxiety. What is the point of bare
breasted women in jeans? I turn the pages quickly.
The blinds are closed, the room air-sealed
like the diving tank on Steel Pier, I remember
as a child: I was always afraid of going under.

The Butcher's Wife

                    The fur,
draped over my grownup shoulders
matted and stiff, like a field
of dry grass, its silk
lining ripped, its patterned leaves
indelible as a Dürer
etching, drifting before the bite
of winter, and her name
embroidered among them, as if

I'm watching a mute commercial
with the ocean's scalloped lip,
cold waves, and an ad
for a funeral
parlor tugged across a gun metal sky
over that small seaside town where
I grew up, the label top
center: *Hoffman Fine Furs Ventnor.*

Drawn to a '50's popular
brown shade, she called *Autumn Haze,*
her rabid brood fixed
unbelieving eyes
on that bright item in a wardrobe
of housedresses and bloodstained white
aprons, the fine mesh
interlining that barely holds

94

the baleful years of family rows,
disintegrating. I never
saw her wear it,
but for a photograph
tableside with Dad at the Latin,
Dad clean shaven, and not raving,
for once! Her alarmed eyes
pop up like the cash register's

black and white numbers: who's watching
the babies in a house of red
carcasses when
a father's heavy
footfalls on the stairs conjures Ivan
the Terrible, and welts rise like
Valentine red hots, no
sugarplum fairies on our minds.

Unloading the Carts

I love to watch the women unloading the metal carts in Sendik's parking lot, they bend over the brown paper bags, filled with leafy produce, milk and cereal, meats and poultry, treats like dried Turkish apricots, preserves from Scotland and France. They fill the trunks of their cars. I think of Millet's peasant women, bending with hoes over the hard ground, their sloping shoulders heavy from the day's work, their long curved arms encircling the earth. They wear their hair bound in white scarves, tied in back of necks graceful as swans'. White dollops of aprons adorn those fruitful laps. It is their job to till the earth, like the women unloading the carts.

Dried Springs

*after Auguste Rodin's Celle qui fut
la belle heaulmière (1840-1914)*

I can understand the women crying for shame, seeing
        her the first time in the Musée Luxembourg, outside

the leaves golden and falling in an eternal autumn. Rodin
        liked naming things *éternelles.* I can see the women,

especially the women, shocked and enthralled, by her abject
        nakedness, rotating around her. I can hear the brushing

of dresses, and underneath, the corseted flesh shouting for
        relief. Hiding their eyes, then peeking through gloved

fingers, to see her large bare hand, its splayed fingers
        reaching across her back, trying to shield her from their

ignominious stares. No nude could be so bare. Her name was
        Caira, an old Italian model, 82, to be precise. Sources

taries or *Dried Springs, Old Woman, Winter,* he called it
        before landing on Villon's poem, *She Who was the Helmet*

Maker's Once Beautiful Wife. Fallen women falling from high
        places. I think Rodin saw a corpse inside every woman.

Which brings me to my mother. Flaccid folds . . . ribs stand out
        between the parchment that covers them . . . the whole

figure seems to totter, to tremble, to shrivel, to shrink
        away. How do we get from the manifold to zero?

The girl running on the beach in the photograph, I have her
        long legs, bony knees, the curved scar on her heel left

by the broken clamshell. Would she know me and love me
        back? I rubbed my old mother's scarecrow legs, trimmed

her fungus ridden nails, placed each weighty breast in a
        brassiere cup, said "you must get up." *The human body is,*

above all, the mirror of the soul, and from the soul comes
        its greatest beauty, said Rodin when he was famous and

liked philosophizing. Like the women, I wanted to turn away,
        but felt my mother's lucent soul and could not deny my own.

Months later shopping for swimsuits with my teenage daughter,
        I see the backs of my legs in the mirror. Veins. *Vanitas.*

A theme for Rodin's composition. *What is commonly called*
        ugliness in nature in art becomes full of great beauty,

Rodin further expounded. When two museum guards walk away
        from *la belle heaulmière,* bantering like Hamlet's grave-

diggers, I touch the face, press into the dark hollows under
        the cheekbones, sink into the cavernous eyes. Trace the

sharp nose, taut thin lips. I remake the veins in her neck,
        spread warm palms against her caved-in chest. Caress the

cold cave of a sunken buttock. Follow the startling fingers
        up to the smooth scapula, hard shiny wings, waiting to fly.

The Anointed

Sunbathing on the stone roof of the beach
house, bikinied teenaged girls and boys
love themselves with suntan oil. Pineapple
and coconut unctions ooze from tubes and clear
plastic bottles. "Lemme" "sez me" "honey,"
they speak in tongues of the promised land,
rubbing each other's out-of-the-way spots,
in back of's, higher up's, above and below
existing landmarks. They gleam like David.

Not far away, there is no shade for me
to lie in, I rub a genie jar of Oil
of Olay, and wish for their radios to stop.
Their supple bodies gyrate like the damned
in a Michelangelo painting. Damn them,
I can't go back to reading. I swat a
fly on my inner thigh; the soft flesh
turns red under a weathered hand. *Mine*.
Not all the oils of Arabia can change that.

End of Summer

And the air changed, a clearing, or
an answer in a cloud series
over the lake. The end
of summer brought relief. Shadows
of maples reared over Lake Drive,
deepening the darker feelings,
but letting joy back. I'd survived
my father's rage, but grief sticks

like a broken wishbone swallowed
in fear of not finishing
the meal. We must all lose
a father, says Uncle Claudius
to Hamlet. Isn't
that what makes life real? The black
backing of the glass? Ourselves
caught in the mirror? What about

that Friday meal? How quickly
the chicken disappears, the neck,
liver, gizzard, the white
meat and dark, the fanned tail part
that skims the fence
last. He liked that, my father,
an empty platter, my half-
eaten young heart.

Pietà Rondanini

Michelangelo Buonoratti 1475-1564

The son leans back on the mother,
his dead naked body shields her
like a god's, and she holds on,
grateful for the child, for the boy
calling her name in the wind.
(Even then he called her Mary.)

Born from shadow into light,
he weighs less now.

Her features are swallowed
by stone, her mantle chiseled
from sorrow, she hugs
his shoulder, her hand dissolves
into his chin, as all form
dissolves into Her.

His limp legs, still beautiful,
fold like a new foal's.

An arm from an aborted work
juts out from his rib:
Art, too, can die and be reborn
from the rubble.

Daniel

When I stole my brother's
Bible stories, I sweated
over exotic names
like so
many intricate knots, untying
each syllable until the words
spun out. *And in the second*
year of the reign
of Nebuchadnezzar who dreamed
bad dreams, Daniel
stepped up to interpret, but
refused to eat *trayf,* upholding
God's reign as unchanging, and
for that was vilified by
the court's sycophants. No more
knots clogged the king's
addled brain, thanks to Daniel's
unraveling. So praise the navel for its orange
dreams issuing from the milk- honeyed words
of my furtive readings — *be fruitful*
and multiply. But Neb's own
Balshazzar, is iced. Who'd carry on
the knots and bolts of the family
business? What's in a name? Isn't
a rose called thorn just
as sweet? Not in your sweet dreams, my
little Dan. *As God is my judge*
is your name, I saw in dreams unfurling
scrolls with beloved names
of the recently
departed, names already
shades when you, first grandchild, were conceived,

words made flesh from children's
fitful dreams for a new
unfettered reign conceived by
hearts unbridled by fearful knots like those
Daniel loosened in the bible where
words delivered us from lions.

Amazing Grace

Cold was the stone slab beneath Luther's
cheeks, as he cursed his belly, swollen under
his cowl like a pregnant woman's. If only
he had faith in the body's wisdom, he might
not be stuck on the privy in this damp
prison of Wittenberg's tower. He ran
his hands over a dome, hard as St. Peter's
and nearly as solid. Was there a rumbling,
a gurgling, any sign of life? He drove
his fists into his spread thighs, grunted,
pushed down, until his other cheeks turned
crimson. All the purgatives in Wartburg
could not stir him. He shifted his weight, leaned
on an elbow and wrestled with doubt: "A dog
squats on its hind legs, deposits its filth
and walks away, wags its tail, justifiably
proud. Why justified, while I sit here, bear down
and give nothing but wind to turn a ship's
sails about?" Unfolding his fists, palms up:
"There with Your grace go I."

Vivaldi and Oranges

I loved the light of course . . . .
    —John Ash

I loved the light, the way
the lake and the sky flirted
with each other on the walls
like a pantomime, or as though
the sea were inside the house.
I loved the house,

the way we lounged on pink couches
in kimonos the color of the sky or the lake,
silks revealing thighs and cleavage,
reminding me of the bathtub paintings
by Bonnard where the light bathes in such profusion
the shadows are bleached out like the despair of his wife
who floats in those paintings; the canvas
always before him tacked to the wall, its ground
blank and scrubbed like the room where Marthe undressed
before entering the green quiet lull of her bath.
I loved the house

where Sundays we lingered in the sunroom over a plate of oranges
    and coffee,
listening to Vivaldi and admiring the wall's antique copy
    of a frieze
of a Roman soldier bowing before his wife, her lips pressed
    to his bare head;
and whether he is taking leave or coming back from a war,
    we could only guess,
knowing that to leave this house would be heroic, that the light
    could fail

as it had before we arrived here, and that we would be drowned
     without it,
but surely like the couple in the relief, we would love each other
     forever . . . .

The house will stand long after the iron gate closes behind
us, and the couples and the joggers who pass back and forth
will look up at the gargoyles and lights, and wonder who lives
here.

The Long Married Life

white drifts outside the window
on the patio like a dream
of white on white the reverse
of Ad Reinhardt's black on black
paintings of those little boxes
when you step up close and look
you think you've seen everything

purple tulips in a vase opening
on a glass top table pedaling
their petals backwards in extremis
showing their blackguard hearts
in time for a Valentine's Day
dinner and I think of the sculptor
Lachaise spreading Isabel until

she's all belly breasts buttocks
and spill I'll serve you salmon
fillets in a lace apron and I
won't dim the lights and afterwards
we'll lie by the fire my hard core
Jim Dine heart pumping on top of
yours truly yours forever

Burrowing from Joyce and Bogan: Unlikely Pairs

I follow the chart
of my body's course
from girlhood's surrender
without remorse,

a trickle it seems
whose source is hidden
above a mountain stream
that comes unbidden

to this widening river.
I see it clear:
the stick figure
becomes a pear,

basque an' jew,
communice and bartlett,
sickleness in heathen,
forrelle, forheign, a hardlot.

Earthly Paradise

after the paintings of Pierre Bonnard

Isn't it what we try for
in our bungling, making
a feast out of a few

fruits and cakes? Yet,
by each frugal dish,
a palpable

grace hovers
over the table, as if
pitchers and plates

were laid to lead us, dear,
through the window into
a garden where a man

and a woman are coming
apart, world between
them: purple bird-

of-paradise, dappled
monkey, mauve rabbits,
even a bluish turkey

The snake's finished,
coiled on a bush above
the woman, a toppled

colossus, blue-vein
marbled; marvelously
corrupted, and the man

stands against a tree, holding
a cigarette between
spread fingers, as he

meditates on the middle
distance. I remember
turning a corner

in the d'Orsay, coming
upon a woman, rather
a painting of her, splayed

in bed, enjoying the body's
utter contentment:
a wide yawn of thighs,

an elbow curled over
a small breast, the other
behind a pillow-bound

head, baring the armpit's
dark hollow, and if I
let you, love, come

closer to me, what beast,
what beast, will crawl
from my menagerie?

The Weight of an Apple

It isn't the Botticelli *Venus* that I remember,
    but the yellow pear I placed on the night table
        for breakfast.

And the muscat grapes' sticky sweetness on my
    fingers, I licked for Donatello's *Magdalene*,
        returned from the desert.

And the roundness and weight of an apple I held,
    watching Giotto's angels weep on the walls
        of the Scrovegni Chapel.

And the brown figs, large as small potatoes, I bought
    from a stall, after passing back and forth
        before the replica of *David*.

And when I bit into the dark cool plum I'd saved
    for the airplane home, I saw the deep
        purple folds in da Vinci's *Annunciation*.

Books Available from Gival Press

A Change of Heart by David Garrett Izzo
1st edition, ISBN 1-928589-18-9, $20.00

A historical novel about Aldous Huxley and his circle "astonishingly alive and accurate."
— Roger Lathbury, George Mason University

An Interdisciplinary Introduction to Women's Studies Edited by Brianne Friel & Robert L. Giron
1st edition, ISBN 1-928589-29-4, $25.00

A succinct collection of articles written for the college student of women's studies, covering a variety of disciplines from politics to philosophy.

Bones Washed With Wine: Flint Shards from Sussex and Bliss by Jeff Mann
1st edition, ISBN 1-928589-14-6, $15.00

A special collection of lyric intensity, including the 1999 Gival Press Poetry Award winning collection. Jeff Mann is "a poet to treasure both for the wealth of his language and the generosity of his spirit."
— Edward Falco, author of *Acid*

Canciones para sola cuerda / Songs for a Single String by Jesús Gardea; English translation by Robert L. Giron
1st edition, ISBN 1-928589-09-X, $15.00

A moving collection of love poems, with echoes of *Neruda à la Mexicana* as Gardea writes about the primeval quest for the perfect woman. "The free verse...evokes the quality and forms of cante hondo, emphasizing the emotional interplay of human voice and guitar."
— Elizabeth Huergo, Montgomery College

Dead Time / Tiempo muerto by Carlos Rubio
1st edition, ISBN 1-928589-17-0, $21.00

Winner of the Silver Award for Translation - 2003 *ForeWord Magazine*'s Book of the Year. This bilingual (English/Spanish) novel is "an unusual tale of love, hate, passion and revenge."
— Karen Sealy, author of *The Eighth House*

Literatures of the African Diaspora by Yemi D. Ogunyemi
1st edition, ISBN 1-928589-22-7, $20.00

An important study of the influences in literatures of the world. "It, indeed, proves that African literatures are, without mincing words, a fountainhead of literary divergence."
—Joshua 'Kunle Awosan, University of Massachusetts Dartmouth.

Metamorphosis of the Serpent God by Robert L. Giron
1st edition, ISBN 1-928589-07-3, $12.00

"Robert Giron's biographical poetry embraces the past and the present, ethnic and sexual identity, themes both mythical and personal."
— *The Midwest Book Review*

Middlebrow Annoyances: American Drama in the 21st Century by Myles Weber
1st edition, ISBN 1-928589-20-0, $20.00

"Weber's intelligence and integrity are unsurpassed by anyone writing about the American theatre today..."
— John W. Crowley, The University of Alabama at Tuscaloosa

The Nature Sonnets by Jill Williams
1st edition, ISBN 1-928589-10-3, $8.95

An innovative collection of sonnets that speaks to the cycle of nature and life, crafted with wit and clarity. "Refreshing and pleasing."
— Miles David Moore, author of *The Bears of Paris*

Prosody in England and Elsewhere: A Comparative Approach by Leonardo Malcovati
1st edition, ISBN 1-928589-26-X, $16.00

"To write about the structure of poetry for a non-specialist audience takes a brave author. To do so in a way that is readable, in fact enjoyable, without sacrificing scholarly standards takes an accomplished author."
—Frank Anshen, State University of New York

Secret Memories / Recuerdos secretos by Carlos Rubio
1ˢᵗ edition, ISBN 1-928589-27-8, $21.00

"From the beginning, the reader feels pulled into the narrator's world and observes, along with him, a delicate, beautiful, and vulnerable universe as personal and intimate as a conversation between lovers."
— Hope Maxell Snyder, author of *Orange Wine*

The Smoke Week: Sept. 11-21, 2001 by Ellis Avery
1st edition, ISBN 1-928589-24-3, $15.00

Writer's Notes Magazine 2004 Book Award—Notable for Culture.
Winner of the Ohioana Library Walter Rumsey Marvin Award
"Here is Witness. Here is Testimony."
— Maxine Hong Kingston, author of *The Fifth Book of Peace*

Songs for the Spirit by Robert L. Giron
1st edition, ISBN 1-928589-08-1, $16.95

This humanist psalter reflects a vision for the new millennium, one that speaks to readers regardless of their spiritual inclination.
"This is an extraordinary book."
— John Shelby Spong, author of *Why Christianity Must Change or Die: A Bishop Speaks to Believers in Exile*

Sweet to Burn by Beverly Burch
1st edition, ISBN 1-928589-23-5, $15.00

Winner of the 2004 Lambda Literary Foundation Award for Women's Poetry; Winner of the 2003 Gival Press Poetry Award
"Novelistic in scope, but packing the emotional intensity of lyric poetry..."
— Eloise Klein Healy, author of *Passing*

Tickets to a Closing Play by Janet I. Buck
1st edition, ISBN 1-928589-25-1, $15.00

Winner of the 2002 Gival Press Poetry Award
"...this rich and vibrant collection of poetry [is] not only serious and insightful, but a sheer delight to read."
— Jane Butkin Roth, editor, *We Used to Be Wives: Divorce Unveiled Through Poetry*

Wrestling with Wood by Robert L. Giron
3rd edition, ISBN 1-928589-05-7, $5.95

A chapbook of impressionist moods and feelings of a long-term relationship which ended in a tragic death. "Nuggets of truth and beauty sprout within our souls."
— Teresa Bevin, author of *Havana Split*

Books for Children

Barnyard Buddies I   by Pamela Brown; illustrations   by Annie H. Hutchins
1st edition, ISBN 1-928589-15-4, $16.00

Thirteen stories filled with a cast of creative creatures both engaging and educational. "These stories in this series are delightful. They are wise little fables, and I found them fabulous."
— Robert Morgan, author of *This Rock* and *Gap Creek*

Barnyard Buddies II   by Pamela Brown; illustrations   by Annie H. Hutchins
1st edition, ISBN 1-928589-21-9, $16.00

"Children's literature which emphasizes good character development is a welcome addition to educators' as well as parents' resources."
— Susan McCravy, elementary school teacher

Tina Springs into Summer / Tina se lanza al verano by Teresa Bevin; illustrations by Perfecto Rodriguez
1st edition, ISBN 1-928589-28-6, $21.00

"This appealing book with its illustrations can serve as a wonderful learning tool for children in grades 3-6. Bevin clearly understands the thoughts, feelings, and typical behaviors of pre-teen youngsters from multi-cultural urban backgrounds...."
— Dr. Nancy Boyd Webb, Professor of Social Work, author and editor, *Play Therapy for Children in Crisis* and *Mass Trauma and Violence*

Inquiries: 703.351.0079
Books available via Ingram, the Internet, and other outlets.
Or Write :
Gival Press, LLC / PO Box 3812 / Arlington, VA 22203
Visit: *www.givalpress.com*

www.ingramcontent.com/pod-product-compliance
Lightning Source LLC
Chambersburg PA
CBHW020913090426

42736CB00008B/612